Never Shag a Scorpio

From Aries to Pisces,
the Complete Astrology
Guide to Dating

Never

a Scorpio

B. J. Lovegood

bantam

TRANSWORLD PUBLISHERS

Penguin Random House, One Embassy Gardens,
8 Viaduct Gardens, London SW11 7BW
www.penguin.co.uk

Transworld is part of the Penguin Random House group of companies
whose addresses can be found at global.penguinrandomhouse.com

First published in Great Britain in 2023 by Bantam
an imprint of Transworld Publishers

A CIP catalogue record for this book
is available from the British Library.

ISBN 9781787637115

Typeset in Masqualero and Hawthorn by Couper Street Type Co.
Printed and bound in Great Britain by Clays Ltd, Elcograf S.p.A.

The authorized representative in the EEA is Penguin Random House Ireland,
Morrison Chambers, 32 Nassau Street, Dublin D02 YH68.

Penguin Random House is committed to a sustainable
future for our business, our readers and our planet. This book is made from Forest
Stewardship Council® certified paper.

To all those who swipe right ...

Contents

Introduction • 2

Aries • 4

Taurus • 16

Gemini • 26

Cancer • 38

Leo • 48

Virgo • 58

Libra • 70

Scorpio • 80

Sagittarius • 92

Capricorn • 102

Aquarius • 114

Pisces • 124

Acknowledgements • 135

Introduction

Since the dawn of time, humanity has turned to the heavens to understand the heart but few could read the signs: Tiberius confused his Pan with his Plough and ended up with Julia the Elder; Nero mistook Polaris for Pyxis and got Sporus castrated; while Kim mixed up Ursa Major with Minor and ended up breaking hearts, not the internet. History is littered with these astrological wrong turns, and it was love that paid the heaviest price.

That was until the end of the fifth century BC, when a cohort of Babylonian astrologers decided to make sense of the heavenly ceiling. They divided the night sky into twelve houses, twelve celestial coordinates that could be used to navigate the ceaseless stirrings of our loins. Since then, these maps have shown us the way: Edwin Hubble spotted his wife's affair from light years away, while Mystic Meg predicted King Charles's canoodling with Camilla long before the *News of the World* got hold of the story. You see, love is written in the stars but we are emotionally illiterate when it comes to reading them.

This is why I have dedicated my life to understanding the twelve planetary profiles – so that you can avoid the pitfalls our ancestors encountered. Armed with my telescope, sundial, binoculars and apps, I have gazed up at the heavens and the stars have revealed themselves to me, showing their fatal flaws, their raging red flags and the hidden gems we so often overlook. After years of first dates and chronic repetitive strain/swiping injury, my research breaks new ground in the world of dating and provides fresh context for your Sunday-night swiping. While love may be blind, you are not. So I implore you to read on, dear reader, read on...

B. J. Lovegood

ARIES

Aries dates: 21 March – 19 April

Element: Fire

Ruling planet: Mars

Preferred pickup territory: Après-ski

Attracted to: High-speed fibre optic broadband

One-night stand rating: 3/10

Favourite sex position: Doggy

Serial-killer vibes: 8/10

Introduces you to their parents after: 2 seconds

Potential ick-factor: 4/10

Preferred dating platform: Chatroulette

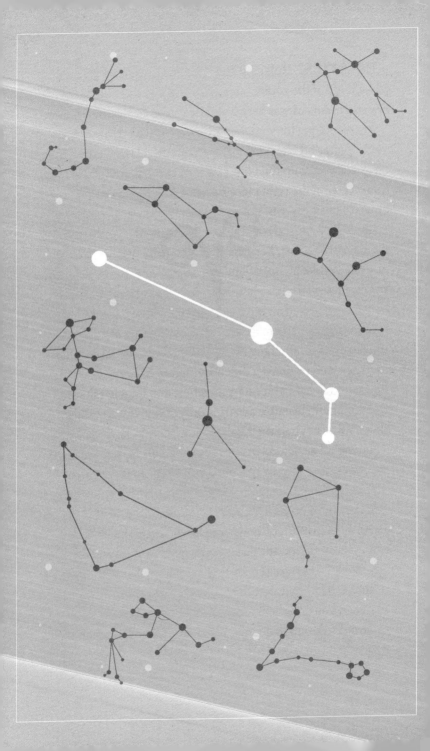

The Aries:

Ruled by Mars, the Aries embodies the raw energy of the zodiac – impulsive, instinctive and highly impatient. An Aries is here for a good time, not a long time. If you're looking for someone to grow old with then perhaps you're better off checking out your old friend the Cancer. If, however, you're up for a one-, two- or even three-night stand, then you're in the right place because Aries wants to get down to business. But not with just anyone.

The Aries' *carpe diem* philosophy means they only want the best of the best, because they *genuinely* believe they deserve it. Like an impatient millennial, they want the finest wines, they want them here and they want them now! You may have guessed already – the Aries is blessed with an ego the size of Saturn. Romantically speaking, this means they're always punching above their weight. Whether these punches land or not is a different matter. Either way, if you find yourself being hit on by an Aries, don't duck, take it as a compliment, because an Aries only shoots for the stars that lie way beyond their galaxy.

Living off a cocktail of ambition and adrenaline, the Aries is never one to shy away from a challenge or adventure. This makes them magnetic leaders and after-party seekers. But they have other uses, too.

If you're just out of a relationship or are feeling a little low on confidence, the Aries is the perfect, no-questions-asked date. They are the ideal rebound; the Samanthas of the zodiac. Their determination to let nothing come between you and them means that an Aries always overlooks the small details. Yes, even your character flaws.

Exploit this to your advantage: so what if you sport boot-cut jeans, are pro-fracking and receive Katie Hopkins's weekly newsletter? The Aries will be blind to all this. For one night you can be your true self – warts and all – and in the morning they'll have left without even a goodbye kiss. Bliss.

Shit where you eat? Being the first sign of the zodiac, Aries are natural-born leaders. Their cocksure nature coupled with their staggering ability to get all things done by ten a.m. means there is plenty of time in the day for some serious office flirting. But watch out: while *Forbes 30 Under 30* is littered with Aries, these colleagues are best admired from a distance. For all their talents and showbiz attractions, their impulsive and somewhat reckless nature means they will lead you astray. While you might be on *their* 'to-do list', they can't always be on the top of yours. If you find yourself in a fling with them, quickly wave goodbye to your objectives for that year.

Typical profession: Bitcoin gambling start-up.

The Aries models themselves on: Elon Musk.

How to flirt with an Aries: Aries are adrenaline junkies, so you need to get their blood pumping. Whisper something risqué in their ear: suggest an al fresco dalliance, inform them that you're not wearing any underwear or tell them you sometimes travel without insurance. If none of these work, simply stab them with an EpiPen. If that fails, take a long hard look in the mirror.

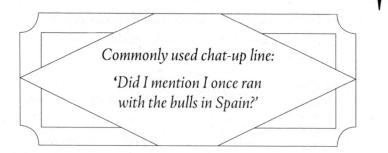

Commonly used chat-up line:

*'Did I mention I once ran
with the bulls in Spain?'*

Preferred method of communication: Texting, while driving.

The relationship history of an Aries: How long have you got? The affairs of an Aries spread through the zodiac like a Californian wildfire. The impulsive Aries means they are both indiscreet and indiscriminate when it comes to finding a mate, which means that, statistically, one in every three of us has slept with an Aries. Let that sink in. Got it? Now get yourself off to the local STI clinic – you'll be guaranteed to find some familiar faces down there ...

Ideal first date with an Aries: For an Aries, there is no thrill more intoxicating than the thrill of the chase. Lean into this as literally as you can:

- Enter a local hide-and-seek championship
- Get tickets to be a contestant on ITV's *The Chase*
- Rewatch Ben Stokes's famous Ashes run chase at Headingley

- Book a table at Dans le Noir? and slip away after one course, leaving them to work out where you've gone

- Ghost them on a semi-regular basis, then invite them round for a spontaneous Netflix and chill session

Split the bill? The Aries' impulsive nature means they are about as fiscally responsible as the Lehman Brothers. The Aries will pick up the bill regardless of whether they can afford it, while refusing to tip on the basis of their belief in trickle-down economics. To avoid having your food spat in on future visits, slip the waiter a tenner on your way out.

How an Aries will flirt with you: Unfortunately for you, an Aries flirts in the manner of their spirit animal, the ram. Like their curly-horned Patronus, the Aries will eye you up and down like you're a ewe in mating season. They will approach you straight on, head down, their hooves raking the earth like an opening batsman eager for runs. This is not an enviable position to be in. Bleat for immediate help. If no one comes to your rescue, simply sidestep their advances by turning your attention to a stranger. The Aries' blinkered approach makes them fairly easy creatures to read and thus avoid.

Sexual appetite: Insatiable. But like a greedy child eyeing up their birthday cake, an Aries' eyes are often too big for their belly. They talk the talk but can they walk the walk?

The answer is usually no. An Aries will channel so much of their energy and enthusiasm into getting you to the bedroom that when you finally arrive there, well, they've already arrived ... Only a fool confuses sexual sophistry with stamina. While many would curl up in shame after such a performance, the Aries will brush this off and, like a Duracell Bunny, immediately suggest going again. Bless them. Gently remind them that slow and steady usually wins the race. If they don't listen, you may have to take matters (quite literally) into your own hands ...

How to tell if an Aries is into you: An Aries possesses as much subtlety as Hagrid after half a dozen butterbeers. They don't play this game by gently dropping hints via friends of friends, or carefully liking Instagram posts on a frequent, but not too frequent, basis. No, the Aries will make their flirtations explicit from the off. The upside of this is that there is no grey area: if it looks like a chirpse, sounds like a chirpse, then yep, you guessed it – you've pulled.

Introduce to your parents: If you can keep them hooked long enough.

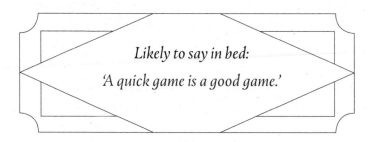

Likely to say in bed:
'A quick game is a good game.'

Best way to break up with an Aries: Tell them you want to take things slowly. The Aries' staggering lack of patience means they're guaranteed to race off for pastures new.

(17:22): Hey, whatcha doing tonight/tomorrow/ this weekend?

(20:37): Hello, I'm good thanks. Just taking it easy, my family are in town atm.

(20:39): So cool that you're into family. I respect that. Next week?

(15:49): Yeah, I could be around, it would be nice to see you again. I should say, I just got out of a bad breakup so I'm keen to take things slow if that's OK with you.

(15:51): You can mourn in the afterlife. Maybe we'll meet there one day. Ciao x #NoTimeWastersPls

**Statistically,
one in every three
of us has slept
with an Aries.
Let that sink in ...**

5 Valentine's gifts
to give an Aries

· • ● • ·

Ethereum

A copy of Reed Hastings's book

BASE jumping lessons

Handcuffs

Xanax
(if you just want a quiet night in)

SHAG/MARRY/AVOID

· • ● • ·

SHAG: *Libra*

MARRY: *Sagittarius*

AVOID: *Virgo*

TAURUS

Taurus dates: 20 April – 20 May

Element: Earth

Ruling planet: Venus

Preferred pickup territory: Motorway service stations

Attracted to: Creature comforts

One-night stand rating: 8/10

Favourite sex position: Cowgirl

Serial-killer vibes: 5/10

Introduces you to their parents after: 5 months

Potential ick-factor: 7/10

Preferred dating platform: The back pages of the *Telegraph*

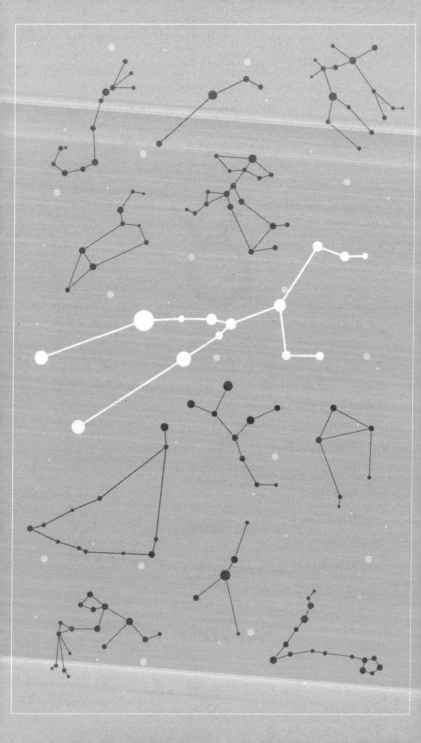

The Taurus:

Part of the earth trio (Taurus, Capricorn and Virgo), the Taurus is the dependable bedrock of the galaxy. They're the North Star. Signified by the bull, the Taurus is – you guessed it – bullish when it comes to matters of the heart, even in a bear market. When they become fixed on something or someone, the Taurus always stays the course.

Dogged and determined, the Taurus is an industrious mule, humbly ploughing their field into perfect geometric patterns. Stoic or stubborn? It's hard to say but it's important to remember that the Taurus isn't difficult on purpose, they just need an overwhelming amount of evidence to alter their point of view. This is both a blessing and a curse. The good news is that the Taurus is no flake. If they say Thursday night at seven p.m., they mean it. They're not going to bail or dither over the question of your place or mine. The downside is that for the Taurus it's either their way or the highway. If you need proof of this, spend a day in the car with them. You will quickly discover their extraordinary ability to be both a back *and* front seat driver simultaneously. Suggest getting the train for any future travel plans.

But there is a flip side to this cognitive quirk. Ruled by Venus, the Taurus is inherently tactile and patient, qualities as rare among the zodiac as they are between the sheets. This makes them the most generous and selfless of lovers. If a job needs doing, always ask a Taurus. Your pleasure is their goal and their staying power guarantees you satisfaction. So there is no need to fake it with a Taurus, or have one anxious eye on the clock. Simply lie back and let the good times roll.

Shit where you eat? The Taurus is the longest-standing employee of any organization. They were here before the fax machine and the pager, they remember when smoking at your desk was actively encouraged, and when women weren't allowed to wear trousers in the office. In short, the Taurus has seen it all. Sadly for you, this means they are alive to the fact that office romances are ill advised (they've learned this the hard way). The Taurus will deflect any romantic advances that come their way and avoid inferred flirtation as if it's the height of the Cold War and HR has the room wired. Make the Taurus your BFF in the office, not your lover. This decision will pay dividends in the long run.

Typical profession: Insurance broker or Jehovah's Witness.

The Taurus models themselves on: Alan Titchmarsh.

How to flirt with a Taurus: If the Taurus is the bull then you have to be the matador. Dress up in your sequins and sparkles and be prepared to dazzle them. Don't make them feel trapped, though, or you might find they start getting aggressive. Let them know that it's just a game. If you want the night to head in a certain direction, then the bull is going to need some serious persuading. Wear them down with a series of flirty jibes until they finally get the picture. Three hours of this and they should be there for the taking.

Commonly used chat-up line:
'I. Like. Your. Face.'

Preferred method of communication: Single-syllable sentences.

The relationship history of a Taurus: They say that loyalty gets you nowhere in life, but does it get you somewhere in love? The Taurus would suggest not. Being a loyal old thing, the Taurus has often remained committed to people who are undeserving of their fidelity. This means they are typically the dumpee rather than the dumper. Deep down there are probably great reservoirs of sadness and mistrust lying within the Taurus, but the fact that they're taking a shot with you speaks volumes to their stoic character. Remember, you can't get back on the horse unless you've fallen off it.

Ideal first date with a Taurus: A Taurus likes to be in the know rather than ambushed by surprises. Send them links with possible suggestions at least a couple of weeks before the date; this will give the glacial creature time to process the options and settle on an outcome. Don't expect your evening to be an impromptu constellation of dive bars or nightclubs. When the Taurus has settled into their cosy nook of a pub there's no moving them. Be prepared to be there until last orders.

Split the bill? The Taurus is famously tight-fisted. You're going Dutch for those opening few months, no two ways about it. If you want to shake things up, play Rock Paper Scissors for the bill. The Taurus's dependable nature will mean they always chose rock. Bless them.

How a Taurus will flirt with you: A Taurus is no emotional Sherlock Holmes so don't expect any subtle negging or coded compliments coming your way. Likewise, don't expect the Taurus to pick up any gentle hints you've been dropping. Instead, they will make their intentions clear through obvious physical gestures. If you're into them, reciprocate. After all, sometimes in life you just have to grab the bull by the horns.

Sexual appetite: Surprisingly high. For all their outdoorsiness and stoic pursuits, the Taurus loves nothing more than a lazy day in bed. Preferably with silk pyjamas and Egyptian cotton sheets. The bull needs constant stroking and feeding and this heavy petting only leads one way. Be warned, though, once the bull starts, they're almost impossible to stop.

How to tell if a Taurus is into you: A Taurus never enters a decision lightly. Even simple questions like 'still or sparkling' demand deep meditation. Consulting the jury of their conscience for all matters great and small, the Taurus

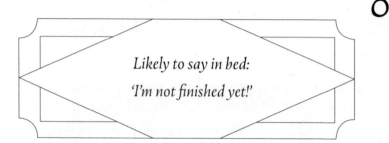

Likely to say in bed:
'I'm not finished yet!'

is not governed by instinct. They will execute thorough background checks on you, scouring your Bebo, Myspace, Facebook and Pinterest for any potential red flags. This intense vetting process means they will have considered you from every angle. Yes, even from down there. If they still like what they see, then their eyes won't wander anywhere else.

Introduce to your parents: To assuage your family's anxiety over your previous unsuitable romantic partners.

Best way to break up with a Taurus: The Taurus's loyal and persevering nature means they will never leave you, no matter how badly you behave. If you want to end things, you're going to have to take things to the extreme. Try hypnotherapy. Failing that, you may have to fake your own death.

(23:07): Hey, it's been great, but I've got loads on at work at the moment and I think I need to focus on myself for a while. It's nothing personal, I just don't think we should see each other any more.

(23:10): I do.

(23:11): Do what?

(23:11): See above.

(08:46): Dinner next week?

Notification (08:47):
'This number has been blocked'

A Taurus's top 5 breakup songs

• • ● ● ● • •

'Grounds For Divorce', Elbow

'Don't Stop Believin'', Journey

'Lean On Me', Bill Withers

'Gotta Get Thru This', Daniel Bedingfield

'I Vow To Thee, My Country',
Gustav Holst and Cecil Spring Rice

SHAG/MARRY/AVOID

• • ● ● ● • •

SHAG: *Scorpio*

MARRY: *Virgo*

AVOID: *Sagittarius*

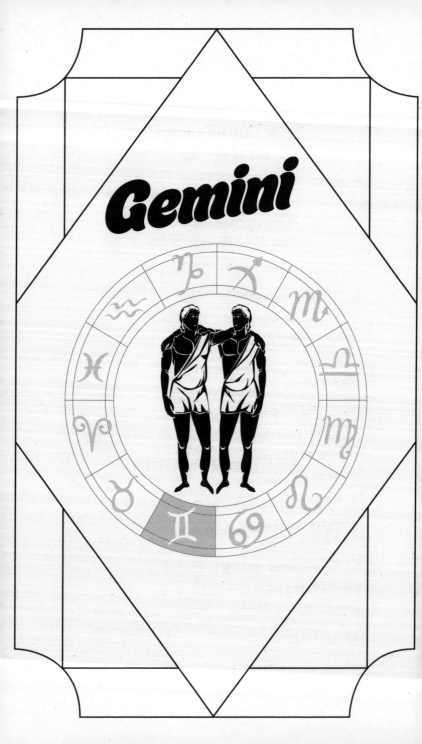

GEMINI

Gemini dates: 21 May – 21 June

Element: Air

Ruling planet: Mercury

Preferred pickup territory: Conceptual art exhibitions

Attracted to: Conspiracy theorists

One-night stand rating: 7.5/10

Favourite sex position: The windmill

Serial-killer vibes: 6/10

Introduces you to their parents: By mistake – they were meant to be out

Potential ick-factor: 7/10

Preferred dating platform: Reddit

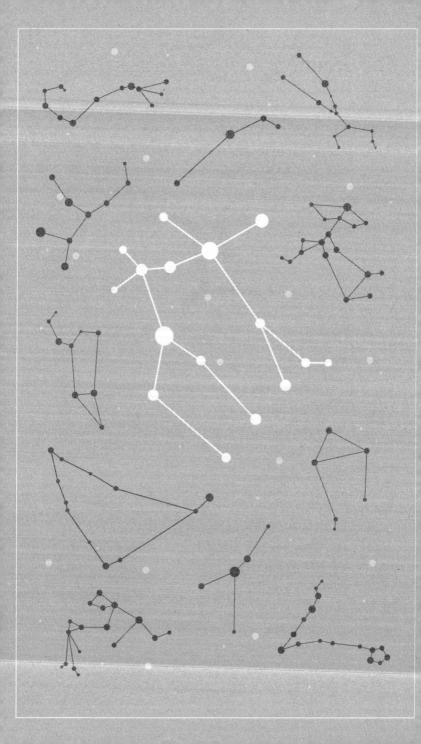

The Gemini: Depicted by twins, the Gemini spells double trouble. If you're dating a Gemini, you've almost certainly bitten off more than you can chew. They are, without doubt, one of the brightest stars in the zodiac. Burning at record temperatures and hurtling through time and space at the speed of light, the Gemini is welcome in every corner of the solar system. Why? Because their company is just too good to go without. Their tireless curiosity and insatiable appetite for the new means that a world of adventure awaits. They are the deep divers, the after-party planners, the wormhole scurriers, the booty-callers. In short, they are a lot. But be warned, these stars can't burn for ever. Eventually they will burn out.

Ruled by Mercury, the Gemini is a twin sign. Now, usually your feet follow your head, but what if you have two heads and they're facing different directions? Like Pisces, the Gemini is a conflicted creature, and it doesn't take a lot for their heads to start turning. Don't freak out – going out with a Gemini isn't like dating Dr Jekyll and Mr Hyde. It's more like taking Jedward on their first UK tour. OK … maybe you should freak out. The point is you need to keep these puppies on a very short leash, otherwise there is no knowing where you'll end up. Be warned, two heads means two faces, so don't be surprised to hear them slagging off the person you thought was their best friend. There is a reason why the Gemini was the biggest gossip in the playground.

But the Gemini is older and wiser now and so are you. Their deplorable childhood traits have now manifested into something far more attractive: they are interested in everything and everyone. Even you. And while they won't fall for any plain Jane, you can guarantee that the Gemini will spot something in you that no one else sees.

Shit where you eat? Being a devout polymath, the Gemini has had more careers than you've had hot dinners. And while their multiple previous professions may sound oh so exciting, the phrase 'Jack of all trades, master of none' was invented for the Gemini sign. Let's be honest, serious questions have to be asked about anyone who has collected ten P45s in as many years. By all means get excited about their professional reincarnations, but if stability is what you're after, move with caution. Remember that a serial entrepreneur is, by definition, a failed entrepreneur. Nod politely as they tell you about their latest start-up venture.

Typical profession: 'Comms . . .'

The Gemini models themselves on: Mary-Kate and Ashley.

How to flirt with a Gemini: Curiosity never killed the cat, but it did get them laid. A Gemini loves to be in the know about anything and everything and the more obscure the topic, the better. They just can't help themselves. Exploit this to your advantage:

- ••● Tell them about your capoeira sessions
- ••● Extol the virtues of your raw-food diet

- State your position on euthanasia in the workplace
- Lay on your love for post-Soviet funk-infused electronica
- Relay the time you went on a bender with Shia LaBeouf

The Gemini will be so overstimulated by these nuggets of conversational catnip that they will become putty in your hand. All you have to do is knead them into shape.

Preferred method of communication: The group chat.

The relationship history of a Gemini: As with postgraduate degrees and Dry January, the Gemini is notoriously good at starting things but not necessarily so good at seeing them through. The same is true of their relationships. For this reason, the galaxy is awash not with old flames but with old embers belonging to the Gemini. The good news for you is that most of these went

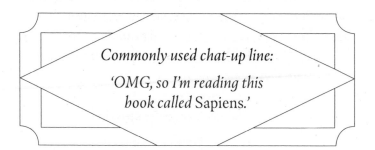

Commonly used chat-up line:

'OMG, so I'm reading this book called Sapiens*.'*

out many moons ago. The bad news is that if a solar wind does suddenly decide to blow, you might find yourself surrounded by fire from all sides.

Ideal first date with a Gemini: A Gemini needs to have all their senses stimulated, preferably all at once:

- Get tickets to a show by Punchdrunk
- Book a tasting menu by Heston Blumenthal
- Make popcorn for hours on end
- Eat sushi off each other's . . .

Split the bill? The Gemini will be so busy talking, they won't have realized the bill has arrived. Don't interrupt them at this point; it will only fluster them. Settle the bill yourself and let the Gemini's ramblings flow. When they eventually notice what you've done, they'll pull out all the stops to pay you back.

How a Gemini will flirt with you: Owing to their Mercurial ruler, Geminis are the social chameleons of the zodiac, and are thus able to flirt with anyone, anywhere, any time. Whether you're at Comic Con or Crufts, the Gemini can get their flirt on. Their key tactic is to find common ground with you as quickly as possible. If you find yourself laughing at an in-joke five minutes after meeting them, the chances are you're the victim of their flirtations. Enjoy it – it's better than most of what else is on the market.

Sexual appetite: Eats anything. Like Alastair Campbell or Rita Skeeter, Geminians are famed throughout the land for their communication skills. This makes them more than exciting company between the sheets. What usually takes place here is a fiery clash between the verbal and the non-verbal. Leave the verbal to the Gemini – they will tell you exactly what they want, how they want you to do it, and how good that makes them feel. And while this might sound rather clinical, like having sex with Siri or Alexa (or both), trust me, it's not. The Gemini's penchant for purple prose will leave you blushing. Leave the dirty talk to them; your job is to focus on the non-verbal. The Gemini is a smooth talker but not the smoothest mover: you're going to have to take the lead on this one and you might even need to whip them into shape – quite literally.

How to tell if a Gemini is into you: A Gemini's attention span blows as quickly as an Aries does in the bedroom. Trying to get them to focus on something for a sustained period of time can be like trying to make Boris Johnson agree to a paternity test. Suggest watching a series

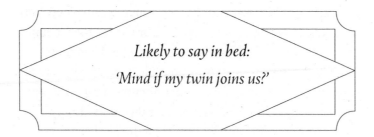

Likely to say in bed:
'Mind if my twin joins us?'

together. If they can get on board until the final episode, chances are they want to get on board you. Either that or the scriptwriting really is superb.

Introduce to your parents: Provided they've had a good sleep the night before.

Best way to break up with a Gemini: Feign ignorance over current affairs. The Gemini will be so put off by your apparent lack of curiosity for the world around you that they will set off for pastures new. Once they've left, start reading the news again.

(14:51): Lololololol

(15:02): What?

(15:02): He's publicly resigned?

(15:38): Who has?

(15:38): For real? Go on the news!

(16:11): Nah, did it once and it just kinda bummed me out. Think I'm better with head in the sand tbh.

(16:21): Pub later?

(19:03): ??

(19:10): I've started seeing someone else. Please respect my privacy at this time. x

Curiosity never killed the cat, but it did get them laid ...

A Gemini's top 5 orgy participants

· · • ● • · ·

Miriam Margolyes

Tyrion Lannister

Dominic Cummings

Cher

Princess Anne

SHAG/MARRY/AVOID

· · • ● • · ·

SHAG: *Gemini*

MARRY: *Aquarius*

AVOID: *Capricorn*

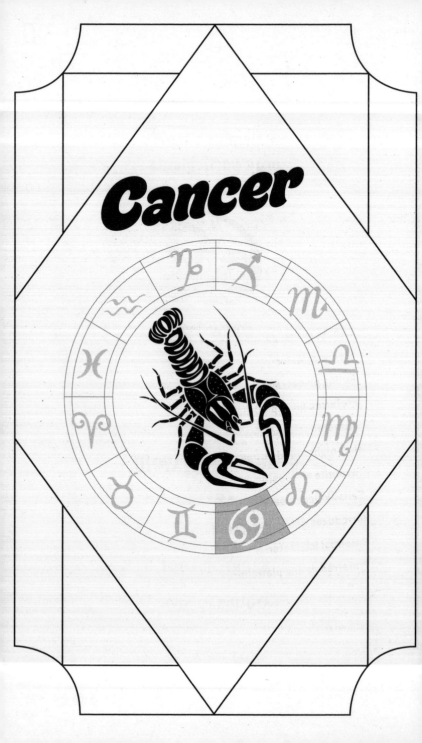

CANCER

69

Cancer dates: 22 June – 22 July

Element: Water

Ruling planet: Moon

Preferred pickup territory: Farmers' market

Attracted to: Emotional damage

One-night stand rating: 7.5/10

Favourite sex position: 69

Serial-killer vibes: 1/10

Introduces you to their parents: On the first date

Potential ick-factor: 6/10

Preferred dating platform: eharmony.com

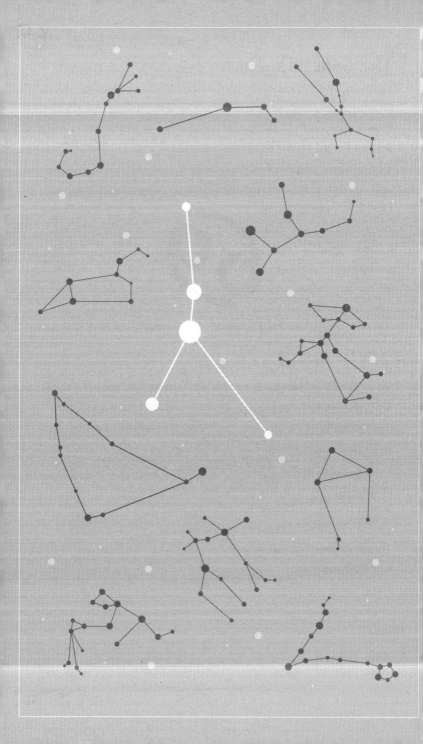

The Cancer: Ruled by the moon, the Cancer is the emotional heartbeat of the zodiac. When you're dating a Cancer, you're guaranteed to experience all the feels. Their submission to the moon means their moods can wax and wane faster than you can say citalopram. Don't let this scare you – it's all part of the Cancer's artistic and emotional temperament. With troughs come peaks. Harness these fluctuations to your advantage; one minute you could be on a quaint country walk, the next dogging in a farmer's field.

But beneath these sudden oscillations, the Cancer is a dependable bedrock of love, loyalty and laughter. This may not always be evident on a first date. Like the crab, the Cancer has evolved to have a hardened exterior. Their ability to hold grudges means that over time layers of resentment slowly build up to form a righteous armour of moral vindication. Don't worry, it's pretty easy to pierce and, as any chef worth their salt will tell you, the crab is worth cracking. Stick with them. Once you get beyond their shell, what awaits you inside is an orgy for the senses.

But for all their supposed complexity, Cancers are surprisingly simple and conservative beings; they are lovers who need loving. Empathetic, creative and caring, ultimately the Cancer just wants to build a life with you. Thinking about it, Cancers are not really crabs, they are simply big wet fish.

Shit where you eat? A Cancer's nurturing nature makes them ideal key workers: they *thrived* during the pandemic. Don't be surprised to hear a Cancer say 'I actually really miss lockdown' long after the vaccine has been rolled out. Striking up an office romance with a Cancer can be a risky business. If you're going to do it, you need to be prepared for what awaits on the other side, because a Cancer isn't leaving their position any time soon. Being allergic to any form of conflict, the Cancer often finds themselves in a professional plateau between the ages of twenty-five and sixty-five, which means you're going to have to get used to them being around long after your dalliance has come to an end. Get accustomed to the awkward lift rides and finding your small talk suddenly becoming as jammed as that paper tray in the HP LaserJet on the second floor.

Typical profession: Children's counsellor or tortured poet.

The Cancer models themselves on: Molly Weasley.

How to flirt with a Cancer: The Cancer hates mind games. For a Cancer, there is no such thing as the thrill of the chase. If you like them, tell them. These comets of clear communication can produce explosive results.

Preferred method of communication: Iambic pentameter.

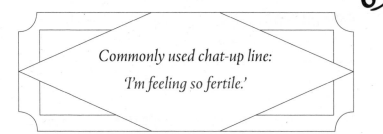

The relationship history of a Cancer: Given their hyper-sensitive nature, a Cancer can hold grudges lasting an eternity. Be warned: if you hurt a Cancer, it's highly likely that you'll end up in their black books for the rest of time. Don't take this too personally – you're in plenty of company. For a Cancer, their old flames never go out; whether they held hands in primary school or poked them once on Facebook, in the eyes of a Cancer these interactions all constitute serious relationships. A Cancer struggles to let go of anything or anyone, so take their number of exes with a pinch, or even a kilogram, of salt and you'll end up with a realistic grip on their romantic past.

Ideal first date with a Cancer: Much depends on what mood they're in. Their *woe is me* tendencies mean they may have got you VIP tickets to a pity party in their local pub. But if the serotonin is flowing then so too are the vibes and you could be in for a night you'll never forget. Remember, Cancers are homebodies, in their element in the safety and comfort of their own nest. Although it sounds vanilla, ask them to cook for you – you'll quickly find that it's only a short hop from the Aga to the bedroom.

Split the bill? The Cancer's highly attuned psychic powers mean they know exactly how much you have in your Monzo account that month. Whether you're skint or flush, they'll call it just right.

How a Cancer will flirt with you: Cancers are funny old fish. OK, they're technically crustaceans, but they *are* funny. Blessed with exceptional mimicry skills, a Cancer's impressions of people can be uncanny. The Cancer is well aware of this and will use the skill to their advantage. If they start their Woody Allen impression, you know they are in peak peacocking mode. Get them to stop immediately. Dating a Cancer can quickly feel like you're watching a poorly dubbed episode of *The Trip* on repeat. Don't let this put you off, though. Allow yourself to be tickled by them and soon you'll be tickling each other in all the right places.

Sexual appetite: Voracious. The best thing about dating a Cancer is their love of eating out. You only have to look at the Cancer's sign to know that they give as good as they get. The Cancer's watery nature means they're quite happy not coming up for air, allowing them to hold a pose for hours on end. Their mastery of this art has earned them Michelin-star reviews from all their old flames.

How to tell if a Cancer is into you: They'll tell you they love you after one pint.

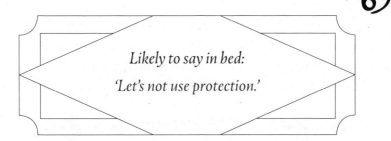

Likely to say in bed:

'Let's not use protection.'

Introduce to your parents: It's never too soon to introduce a Cancer to the family. Sunday lunch is where they come alive. Before you can say 'pass the gravy', the empathetic Cancer will have ingratiated themselves as part of the family furniture, discussing the menopause with your mother and getting your father to open up about his distant relationship with *his* father. Beware, the Cancer may soon mistake your family for their own. For optimum relationship results, limit these meetings to once or twice a year.

Best way to break up with a Cancer: Tell them the thought of marriage and children appals you. The Cancer will be so horrified by this, and relieved to have sidestepped this potential family-less future, that they will feel positively ecstatic that things have ended.

21 Oct 2022

(11:41): Hey, sorry about last night. I was just trying to be honest. I've thought about it a lot and I know I just don't want to have kids. It's not who I am and I don't think I can change that. I'm sorry.

(12:34): I'm in pieces. Life is our gift to pass on. My soul needs a counterpoint, someone to let the mighty river of life pass through.

(14:55): OK. You do you, hun x

11 July 2025

(07:29): Hey!! Long time no speak! Hope you're really well. This might sound totally out of the blue but would you like to be godparent to my child? I think you would be the best role model. Anyway, let me know. Baby is due in three weeks!

(10:46): No worries if not, obvs x

A Cancer's top 5 baby names

• • ● • •

Margot

Quentin

Ophelia

Ernest

Wilbur

SHAG/MARRY/AVOID

• • ● • •

SHAG: *Pisces*

MARRY: *Taurus*

AVOID: *Capricorn*

LEO

Leo dates: 23 July – 22 August

Element: Fire

Ruling planet: Sun

Preferred pickup territory: Gryffindor common room

Attracted to: The limelight

One-night stand rating: 9/10

Favourite sex position: Shower sex

Serial-killer vibes: 2/10

Introduces you to their parents after: An awards ceremony

Potential ick-factor: 8/10

Preferred dating platform: Inner Circle

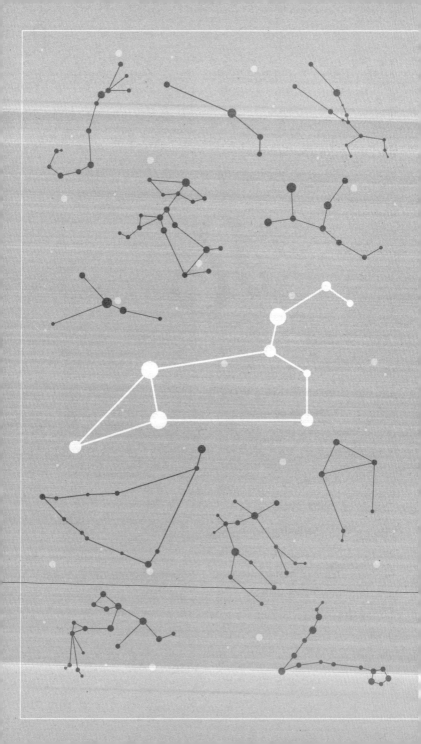

The Leo: We love to hate a Leo. If you don't hate a Leo you're missing out on a lot of fun because there is simply so much to hate. From their good looks, to their insufferable LinkedIn posts, down to their unwavering moral compass, the Leo is the prodigal son of the zodiac. They are the Meghan Markles, the Madonnas, the Ben Afflecks of the galaxy, the ones for whom the stars just seem to fall into line. So why do we hate them? Well, if we're being honest with ourselves, it's because we're jealous. They are the overachievers and we . . . well, we're just like all the rest – staring up at them from the gutter.

Ruled by the sun, the Leo is the centre of the universe. The star around which the rest of us revolve. To be fair, someone has to take up this position in the solar system and we should be grateful it's the Leo because they *own* it. Loud, proud and full of *joie de vivre*, the Leo is the giver of energy and life. And while they always help others to achieve their goals, their own achievements invariably outshine everyone else's. Living off a strict diet of PMA (positive mental attitude), for the Leo nothing is impossible. This makes them exceptional leaders and is the reason they are depicted as the lion – they are the ruler of the pack.

But while lions are all well and good, they are not infallible. Imagine waking up next to Aslan's righteousness every day. You'd start longing for him to fall into the hands of some illegal poachers. That said, dating a Leo is an accolade in anyone's crown. But the Leo has a fatal flaw. For all the lion's wisdom, they have yet to learn that Mr or Ms Perfect does not exist. And while it's flattering to think you are this in their eyes, eventually they will work out you

are not. Then they will start wandering the plains alone, in search of perfect pastures new, the happy times you once shared nothing more than a memory. That greener grass, nothing more than a mirage . . .

Shit where you eat? Striking up an office romance with a Leo is a bold move – not least because the Leo will inevitably be the head of the organization you work for. Shagging the boss is a risky play and, given their status, they will have more to lose than you have to gain (unless you're Matt Hancock). You're playing with fire – but fire is hot, so it's understandable that you want to go there. But be prepared for the office rumour mill to churn into overdrive, expect clandestine conference calls popping into your calendar and off-site work trips with clients you've never heard of. There's no denying the thrill, but this sort of romance usually ends in disgrace. My advice would simply be not to go there. Instead, imagine what could be from the safety of your desk – their PowerPoint sliding into your inbox . . . Some fantasies are best left as just that.

Typical profession: The founder of a dynamic renewable energy company, where all the staff are paid equal six-figure salaries.

The Leo models themselves on: The Obamas.

How to flirt with a Leo: Leos are used to being the centre of attention. They crave the audience's applause, having roses hurled at their feet, the audience rising to an

ovation ... and while you might want to give them this, don't. At least initially. Take them down a peg or two with a few cutting remarks. Deliver them with a smile, though. You want to poke the lion's pride, not wound it indefinitely. A few perfectly timed zingers at their expense will make the lion roar in all the right ways.

Preferred method of communication: Via tasteful, but somewhat extravagant, gifts. Hand-delivered by their secretary.

The relationship history of a Leo: Being a devout disciple to the chivalrous code that a gentleman or woman never tells, discovering the Leo's old flames can be like getting blood from a stone. Unlike the Virgo, who has nothing to tell, the Leo has plenty of skeletons in their closet. It's just that they're buried so deep you have to wade halfway to Narnia to unearth them. If you do manage to excavate one, don't expect the Leo to dish any dirt on them. They treat all their ex-lovers with the same grace and respect they do you. While this hardly makes you feel special or different to the rest, take comfort in knowing that

Commonly used chat-up line:
'Would you like an autograph?'

you could well be joining them in the future, and wouldn't it be lovely to be described in such a flattering light?

Ideal first date with a Leo: When you're choosing a venue, you need to pick somewhere that can accommodate the Leo's BDE. Think full-bodied wines, a kilo of tomahawk steaks, quadruple espressos, black-and-white pictures on the wall – you know the places I'm talking about, the ones with a brass band in the corner and a maître d' who knows you by name. The intensely full-flavoured atmosphere of the place will make the Leo rise to the occasion, spoiling you with charming anecdotes and romantic gestures that are unequivocally slick.

Split the bill? Don't be silly. The Leo is such a charming and loyal creature, and so friendly with local restaurant owners and their staff, that when they enter the establishment they will be greeted like a long-lost child. Their request for the bill will be waved away in mocking disbelief, insisting that it's on the house. This may or may not be an elaborate charade where the Leo actually settles up with the restaurant owner the next day via PayPal, but who cares? Enjoy the theatre of it all.

How a Leo will flirt with you: A Leo is not shy when it comes to big gestures. In fact, they're somewhat 'Hollywood' in their courting habits. Watch out – firework displays, hot-air balloon rides and Christmas markets could well await. If this doesn't ring your bell, you might not want to open the door when they're standing on your lawn holding aloft a boom box. Aim your vomit where you please.

Sexual appetite: Never-ending. The Leo is the carnal carnivore of the dating kingdom. Their alpha nature means they've made it their mission to become a maestro in the bedroom. Abiding by Malcolm Gladwell's philosophy that you need to spend ten thousand hours at something in order to become a master of it, the Leo is up for nookie morning, noon and night. Ruled by the flames and the sun, you're guaranteed a fiery encounter between the sheets with a Leo. So lube up with some SPF and enjoy those sweet, sweet rays.

Likely to say in bed: 'Pull my mane.'

How to tell if a Leo is into you: They dedicate the first volume of their published memoir to you, aged thirty-three.

Introduce to your parents: If they don't mind becoming tabloid fodder.

Best way to break up with a Leo: Book an off-grid romantic retreat for the two of you. The thought of eating an acai bowl in a hot tub post-workout without being able to post it on Insta will send them running for the hills.

(10:31): Hey bbz, why haven't you liked my most recent post? 🤔

(10:51): Work is mad. Which post are you talking about?

(10:52): You don't have notifications for me turned on?

(11:14): No, I have a life instead.

(11:44): I actually really respect that. And because I respect that so much, I think I should give your life the space and respect it needs to flourish. It's been a blast. All my best x

5 lines that will turn off a Leo

· · • ● • · ·

I haven't actually listened to your podcast

Can you introduce me to your friend?

I get really bad imposter syndrome

Shall we take the bus?

Your flat is so cute and small!

SHAG/MARRY/AVOID

· · • ● • · ·

SHAG: *Aries*

MARRY: *Libra*

AVOID: *Pisces*

VIRGO

Virgo dates: 23 August – 22 September

Element: Earth

Ruling planet: Mercury

Preferred pickup territory: Evening MA courses

Attracted to: Chastity

One-night stand rating: 2/10

Favourite sex position: The spoon

Serial-killer vibes: 7/10

Introduces you to their parents after: The sixth mass extinction

Potential ick-factor: 5/10

Preferred dating platform: The *Guardian* online

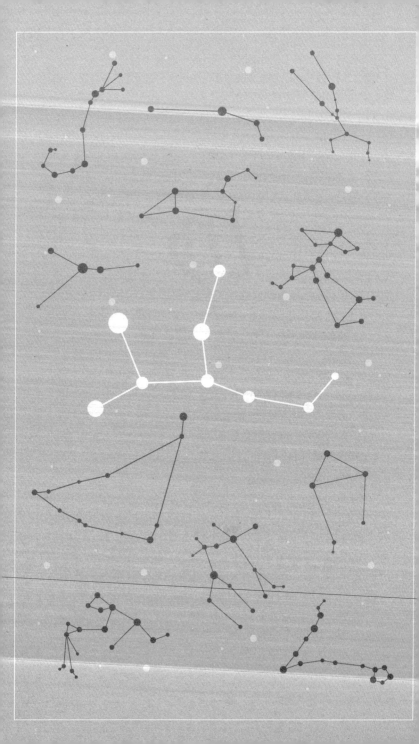

The Virgo: Symbolized by the Virgin, the Virgo is the disappointed goddess of the galaxy. Disappointed not just in others, but also in their own lack of luck concerning matters of the heart, though there is reason to believe that they only have themselves to blame. Cool, reserved and highly intelligent, the Virgo is one of the most perceptive signs of the zodiac. A first encounter with a Virgo can often be an intimidating affair: their economy with words, refusal to suffer fools and ability to suss you out from an alarming distance makes them quite frosty company. You see, Virgos are perfectionists and nothing passes beneath their radar. While this makes them excellent proofreaders or CCTV monitors, it also means they can see the worst in everyone – which doesn't make for a colourful dating life. Hence, their virginal status. Trying to coax a Virgo into bed is like trying to explain the solar system to a flat earther. And while this chaste philosophy is all well and good, Virgos would have considerably more fun on this planet if they were reminded that their time here is finite.

By now you may be imagining they're all doom and gloom, but this is not the case. Spend some time with a Virgo and you will slowly discover the riches of their personality. Their ability to love unconditionally is unmatched in the zodiac, and their self-sacrificing nature means they are constantly putting the needs of others before their own. In this respect they share the Cancer's martyrish ways but, unlike the Cancer, the Virgo is not martyrish about being a martyr. They just quietly get on with it, like William Tyndale or Prince Harry.

If you're looking for a one-night stand, you're wasting your time with a Virgo. You need to have patience – preferably that of a saint. And while the Virgo is slow to thaw, their meltwater is definitely worth sticking around for.

Shit where you eat? No matter how attracted you are to the Virgo, no matter how perfect you may imagine this coupling to be, it's never – and I repeat, never – going to happen in the workplace. The Virgo is any line manager's dream; they are the teacher's pet – organized, practical and exceptional at taking minutes. They are unequivocally hot professional property and the reason that any company belongs in FTSE 100 is because their workforce is made up primarily of Virgos. The Virgo takes immense pride in their work and leads by example. They go hard in the boardroom, but not in the way you're hoping. If you want it to happen between you and a Virgo, you need to ask them for their number and your P45 at the same time.

Typical profession: Judge at the Old Bailey.

The Virgo models themselves on: The Virgin Mary.

How to flirt with a Virgo: For all their merits and undeniable qualities, the Virgo is their own harshest critic. Their self-flagellatory pursuits have led them to develop a chronic case of imposter syndrome, which extends to their romantic life. Your job on the date is to make them feel confident in themselves:

- Compliment them on their appearance

- Laugh at their jokes, even if they're not funny

- Give them your full attention – leave your phone on flight mode or, better still, smash it to pieces in front of them

- Reveal a little vulnerability

- Again, laugh at their jokes. *Please* laugh

Complete the above and you will find their imposter syndrome gradually morphing into a healthy level of Stockholm syndrome. Lean in.

Preferred method of communication: Pen pals, developing a steady correspondence over a three- to five-year period.

The relationship history of a Virgo: The Virgo's chaste nature means that their relationship history is such a non-event in the tapestry of time, a period so devoid of

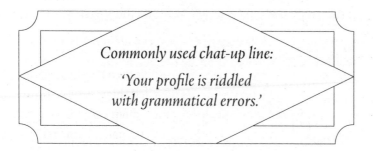

Commonly used chat-up line:

'Your profile is riddled with grammatical errors.'

sexual drama and scandal, that historians have renamed it 'the sexual extinction age', where the birth rate was nil and human life came to a grinding halt.

Ideal first date with a Virgo: The Virgo will not swoon to the tune of chichi bars or swanky new restaurants; they are too down to earth for this. Virgos are the ideal dating partner to have in January because, as dates go, they're as cheap as chips and will enjoy any of the below:

- A walk in the park
- Catching up on Zoom
- 2 for 1 cinema tickets
- A free exhibition
- Staring at clouds

Whatever you do, just don't be late or bail on them last minute. Doing so will ensure you're consigned to the Virgo's black books for ever.

Split the bill? 100 per cent. The Virgo's crusade for fairness, equality and justice is never made more manifest than when it comes to splitting the bill. In the eyes of the Virgo, everyone should pay their fair share. This is fine if it's a dinner *à deux*, a simple case of 50/50, but if you're in a larger group, be warned. The Virgo is the first to insist that because they didn't have a starter and barely touched the sharing platter, everyone should pay individually. Spare a thought for the waiter and their mental maths as all the fun quickly evaporates from the evening.

How a Virgo will flirt with you: While the Virgo may be aloof, this distant vantage point allows them to get a clear oversight of you, the setting and all the bullshit that is tumbling out of your mouth. These powers of perception, paired with a wit drier than a seaman's biscuit, mean the Virgo can deploy the zingiest of zingers. If you start to feel all too seen by the Virgo's cutting comments, it's because they have the eyes for you.

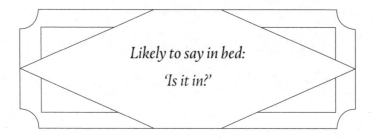

Likely to say in bed:

'Is it in?'

Sexual appetite: Measly. Literary scholars have now confirmed that when Andrew Marvell wrote those renowned opening lines of 'To His Coy Mistress' – 'Had we but world enough, and time, This coyness, lady, were no crime' – he was, in fact, directly addressing the Virgo. The Virgo's virginal status makes them a tough nut to crack but the rewards are there for those prepared to take a longer-term view. Virgos are like Pringles – once you pop, you can't stop.

How to tell if a Virgo is into you: They will have pointed out all your flaws, from your bad breath to your cringe chat-up lines, to the skid marks in your underpants. If they're prepared to hang out with you despite all of these, they probably think you're a good egg.

Introduce to your parents: If your parents like being judged.

Best way to break up with a Virgo: Appeal to their martyrish ways. Knowing they will be forfeiting your relationship to an injustice beyond their control will make them feel deeply righteous and rewarded.

(13:08): Guess what, I've been summoned for jury service!

(13:11): No way! What's the case?

(13:15): They mentioned something about asylum seekers. They said the trial could last for two weeks.

(13:17): Gosh. Although it breaks my heart, I think this is where we should part ways. Justice must come before my wants and needs. The people deserve you more than I do.

(13:22): Huh? It's only two weeks . . .?

(13:29): Please, don't make this harder than it needs to be.

Virgos are like Pringles – once you pop, you can't stop

5 ways to coax a Virgo into bed

· · • ● • · ·

Explain that sex is free

Show them just how quickly the ice caps are melting and that we're all going to die

Feed them oysters incessantly

Promise them you love them

Remind them it is your wedding night after all

SHAG/MARRY/AVOID

· · • ● • · ·

SHAG: *Scorpio*

MARRY: *Taurus*

AVOID: *Capricorn*

LIBRA

Libra dates: 23 September – 22 October

Element: Air

Ruling planet: Venus

Preferred pickup territory: Outside a small-claims court

Attracted to: Approval

One-night stand rating: 8.5/10

Favourite sex position: The spread eagle

Serial killer vibes: 1/10

Introduces you to their parents after: Careful deliberation

Potential ick-factor: 3/10

Preferred dating platform: Hinge

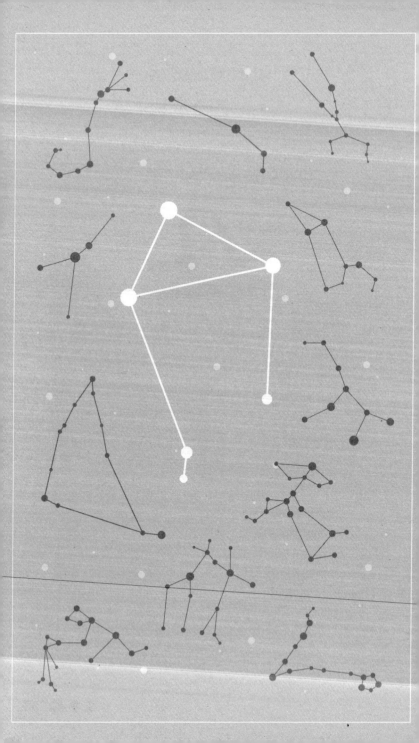

The Libra:

Libra is in the house of marriage.
Principled, diplomatic and an emitter of love, a Libra is
someone you need to have around. When chaos reigns and
tempers flare, the Libra is always called upon to be keeper
of the peace, the calmer of the storm. They are Valium
incarnate. Open and kind, the Libra is prepared to consider
everyone's point of view and will move mountains to make
sure everyone is heard and assuaged. Imagine if LBC Radio
and the fairy godmother had a love child – this would be
the Libra.

Symbolized by the scales of justice, a Libra is out to
ensure the equilibrium of the galaxy. Balancing the push
and pull of cosmic forces, they want the atmosphere around
them to be one of harmony and peace. Relationships are
crucial to this. The Libra will see their chosen partner as
the balancing force in their life, the yin to their yang, the
cucumber to their Hendrick's. But while the Libra expends
much of their energy ensuring that everyone else is settled
and assured, they often overlook themselves in this
equation and are left, ironically, out of kilter.

When it comes to the world of dating, a Libra is nothing
but vibes. Their ruling planet of Venus makes them sexy
and social company, while their penchant for aesthetics
means they always walk through the door sporting the
latest trend. Cue the turning of heads, yours included.
However, after a long day of keeping the peace, often the
Libra just wants to throw their hands up and say 'fuck it'.
If you catch them during one of these moods, you could be
the 'it' they fuck.

Shit where you eat? The Libra is an open-minded soul who is prepared to listen to everyone's point of view on topics ranging from social media strategy, to forecasts for the financial year, to starting an office romance with you. If you think there is a compelling business case for the stirrings in your loins, then the Libra is all ears. Book a meeting room and put the case to them. But remember, the Libra is all about the work-life balance. They've worked hard to achieve that elusive equilibrium, so factor this in to any proposal you put to them:

- Suggest rebranding your weekly catch-ups as something more ... spicy
- Point out that any romantic dates could be filed as a work expense
- Note that WFH in bed together would be a highly efficient way of streamlining your comms

Typical profession: Foreign diplomat or a gong bath therapist.

The Libra models themselves on: Princess Diana.

How to flirt with a Libra: It sounds obvious, but the answer is by flirting. I don't mean sending a suggestive vegetable emoji on WhatsApp, I mean actually flirting. Why? Because the Libra is unapologetic in their love for this lost art, and – let's be honest – it *is* an art. The well-timed touch, the cheeky grin, the sparkling back and forth – it's a dance we wish more people knew the moves to. Satisfy this desire, engage them in eye contact, dabble with some unconscious footsie, let that comment linger a little too long... But remember, it's all about balance with them. Tilt your actions into the realms of cringe and cheese and the Libra will run a mile. Play it cool. If in doubt, just smile.

Preferred method of communication: Group therapy.

The relationship history of a Libra: Plentiful. The Libra is the most lovable sign of the zodiac – and for good reason: they are lovers of love. The ruling planet of Venus means that these stars have always burned for romance. As a result, they have a back catalogue of ex-lovers set to rival that of Drew Barrymore. While none of these should be cause for alarm, the Libra's need for harmony and peace means they are still friends with all their exes, so most of them are still in the picture. But don't worry, they are firmly in the background.

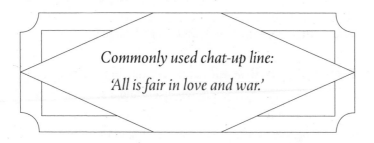

Commonly used chat-up line:
'All is fair in love and war.'

Ideal first date with a Libra: The Libra's optimistic dating disposition makes them a rare breed. While most of us see dating as an arduous and expensive ritual we have to undergo in order to get on the property ladder and have someone to pay for our palliative care in later life, the Libra genuinely loves it. So don't fuck it up. The Libra will bring none of that all-too-common pragmatic caution to the table – there will be no question marks over how late they should stay out or whether they should risk wasting a perfectly good Thursday night on the unknown entity that is you. No, the Libra will come armed with nothing but good vibes. You have no idea how rare this is. Match them toe to toe, put on your glad rags and your smiliest face and throw yourself in head first.

Split the bill? Obvs. The Libra's totem isn't the scales of justice for no reason – financial fairness is the name of their game. This isn't even a conversation. You're going Dutch.

How a Libra will flirt with you: Full of questions and in need of answers, the Libra will bombard you with a flurry of excited enquiries. By the end of the date you'll have answered so many queries that the Libra will know you better than you know yourself. Feeling slightly dizzy from it all, you'll only gradually come to realize that the Libra has steadily edged their way into your inner orbit.

Sexual appetite: Rapacious. The ruling power of Venus means that Libra's sexual pull is strong, making them excellent company in the bedroom. Their highly social nature and people-pleasing tendencies make them no stranger to an orgy, either. If there is a party going on at a Libra's house, then everyone is invited. However, the Libra's need to ensure everyone has a good time can mean they forego their own pleasure in the bedroom. This is where you need to step up. Invite the Libra to surrender themselves to the moment, using some light bondage if you have to. Taking control will hit their indecisive G spot like nothing else.

How to tell if a Libra is into you: They introduce you to all their exes.

Introduce to your parents: If they're going through a divorce. The Libra will act as the perfect mediator.

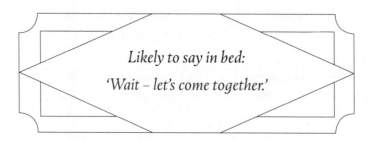

Likely to say in bed:
'Wait – let's come together.'

Best way to break up with a Libra: You can't – not entirely, at least. The Libra's insistence on being friends with all their exes means that any breakup is going to be on good terms, no matter how badly you have behaved.

(10:52): Once again, I am so so sorry – the way I behaved is inexcusable. You deserve so much more and so much better. I'm truly truly sorry.

(11:36): I appreciate the apology. And while you cheating on me with several people simultaneously over a six-month period when we've been going out for three years and we live together is beyond disrespectful, I understand why. I know I'm not the easiest company sometimes and I appreciate that you've a lot of growing still to do and a lot of people you want to meet. I don't see this as a reflection of your true nature, only a blip in what has been a difficult episode in your life, especially with what's happened at work and at home. We're all human and although we make mistakes, mistakes are part of the journey to becoming the people we want to be. Take care and please be kind to yourself. Also, fancy going laser questing next week? X

Top 5 dates for a Libra

• • ● • •

Salsa dancing

Life-drawing class

Day rave at a secret location

Volunteering at a soup kitchen

A swingers' party

SHAG/MARRY/AVOID

• • ● • •

SHAG: *Leo*

MARRY: *Gemini*

AVOID: *Cancer*

SCORPIO

Scorpio dates: 23 October – 21 November

Element: Water

Ruling planet: Mars and Pluto

Attracted to: Their best friend's partner

Preferred pickup territory: Soho House

One-night stand rating: 9/10

Favourite sex position: Anything involving a swing

Serial-killer vibes: 10/10

Introduces you to their parents after: 4 months

Potential ick-factor: 8/10

Preferred dating platform: Raya

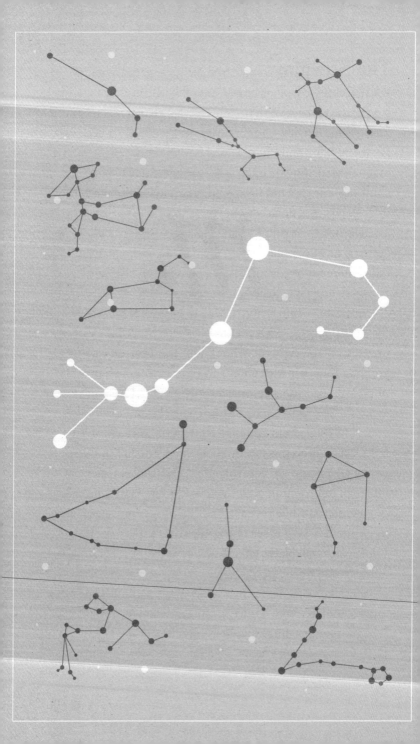

♏

The Scorpio: Tread carefully, for you have been warned. The Scorpio is unquestionably the most dangerous sign in the zodiac. With their mercurial charm and magnetic impulse for fun, few can resist the Scorpio's advances. Ruled by Mars and Pluto, Scorpios are intense pleasure magnets. Hurtling through lovers at breakneck speed, these shooting stars are fun to ride but often lead you to a galaxy of darkness and destruction.

Together, their ruling planets form a celestial cocktail of cunning and coercion. After all, the sting in the Scorpio's tail is there for a reason: love is a game to be won and Scorpios don't like losing.

Dating a Scorpio is like talking to your therapist, only they're plying you with cocktails and desperate to perform oral sex on you right there and then. The Scorpio will lure you into their lair with charm and a relentless volley of intense and all-too-personal questioning. Before you've even finished your (first) negroni, you'll somehow find your darkest secrets tumbling from your lips and into their lap. Don't worry, this is entirely normal. The Scorpio's desire for power and control means they will tease every ounce of information out of you until there is nothing left to give, all the while revealing nothing of themselves. This is intentional. Two glasses of organic wine and a selection of European small plates later, a power dynamic has formed. This is when the Scorpio strikes.

What happens next is nearly always fun; the Scorpio's intense and extreme nature means you're in for a night you won't forget in a hurry and neither will your group chat. But be careful now – while it might have been thrilling to surrender yourself to the Scorpio, their obsessive and possessive nature means that if they like you, they won't let you go in a hurry. At this point you need to make a choice, because half measures aren't on the menu. The Scorpio is either in or they're out. And trust me – you'll know when they're in.

Shit where you eat? While it's never wise to dip the pen in company ink, some documents need a signature. To new joiners, the Scorpio is undeniably attractive in the workplace: well dressed and well groomed, and oozing strategy and charm. They are the first to sidle up to senior partners at the office party, join in with conversations about golfing handicaps and pretend to be interested in colleagues' children. Flirtatious and fun, the Scorpio will make a point of talking to all employees great and small – even you. But long-standing employees will know not to be fooled by the Scorpio's everyman charm; beneath their convivial manner and sparkling water-cooler chat, the Scorpio is an operator. Their suggestion of lunch, or drinks, or brainstorming in the breakout room, is code for one thing and one thing only – they want to get you into bed. But there is always a catch. There always is with a Scorpio. In the post-coital pillow talk they will steal your contacts and your PowerPoint slides, and work out when you're going on parental leave. You see, the Scorpio is the shark of the office ocean, the apex predator of the Square Mile. Their goal is to consume all those who come between them and the boardroom. So be warned, whatever happens between you and the Scorpio is strictly business. Come performance-review time, they will be the first to let you know what the underside of a bus looks like.

Typical profession: Estate agent or international arms dealer.

The Scorpio models themselves on: Logan Roy.

How to flirt with a Scorpio: Nothing stimulates a Scorpio more than a challenge. Succumb to them too quickly and it's unlikely they'll want you to come again. When dating a Scorpio, you need to prey upon their fixed zodiac quality; a Scorpio never gives up the chase. Exploit their relentless nature to your advantage; string them out and string them along. Learn to play with your food before you eat it. See how far you can push this:

- Bail on them last minute
- Say you're going to a seven-day festival without any phone signal
- Emigrate temporarily
- Pretend to want to focus on yourself for a while
- Say you're giving up physical contact for Lent

Evading the Scorpio's stinger will only serve to heighten their infatuation. Feigning disinterest to a Scorpio is like a red rag to a bull; taunt them and tease them for as long as you dare. Eventually they'll buckle and kneel before you.

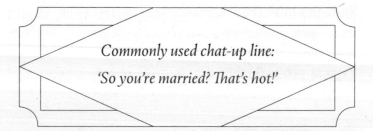

Commonly used chat-up line:
'So you're married? That's hot!'

Preferred method of communication: Voice notes at three a.m. Sober.

The relationship history of a Scorpio: The zodiac is lit up with the Scorpio's old flames. Wherever the Scorpio goes, they leave a burning trail of destruction in their wake. Like the surface of the sun, the Scorpio's love life is a series of intense and fleeting romantic combustions. Ex-lovers are left burned and a little motion sick. This dizzying constellation of sexual explosions can all be mapped back to a romantic black hole that lies just beyond Jupiter – aka the one that got away. Rest assured, you'll never hear about them. The Scorpio's ability to conceal their vulnerabilities in a vacuum of dark matter is one of their greatest strengths.

Ideal first date with a Scorpio: Don't even bother suggesting a venue; the Scorpio will have pre-planned a series of romantic booby-traps to overwhelm and ensnare you. These commonly take the form of contrived and well-documented speakeasy bars, hidden behind doors posing as bookshelves in suspiciously swanky venues. Enter at your peril.

Split the bill? The Scorpio will have discreetly settled this at some point during the evening without you knowing. This smooth and generous move is the Scorpio's way of ensuring you are in their debt from day one. Alert your bank immediately.

How a Scorpio will flirt with you: Never look a Scorpio directly in the eye. Blessed with dangerously poisonous retinas, the eyes of a Scorpio are their most bewitching asset. The Scorpio knows this and will seek to maintain intense eye contact with you at all times, even in the back of an UberPool. Navigating the sexual advances of a Scorpio is akin to fending off the gaze of the Basilisk or Medusa. They have the ability to undress you without even blinking. To offset the effects, stare over the Scorpio's shoulder once every minute, and if you find their gaze wandering to lock on to yours, know the Scorpio has you in their sights.

Sexual appetite: Outrageous. When it comes to being a dom or a sub, there is only one answer with the Scorpio. A Scorpio's need to dominate and control is made manifest in the bedroom. Don't be surprised if you enter a Scorpio's bedroom only to be confronted with more than just their body. Whips, chains, handcuffs and toys are all to be expected in the Scorpio's lair. But don't let that put you off. The Scorpio's tools are all in the name of adventure and fun (and good taste). It's more Killing Kittens than Max Mosley's birthday party. The Scorpio's desire to push each moment to its extreme means you're in for a wild ride. So pack your marigolds and remember to establish a safe-word before you get down to business.

Likely to say in bed: 'That plug isn't for the sink.'

How to tell if a Scorpio is into you: They send you unsolicited nudes via LinkedIn.

Introduce to your parents: The Scorpio will be desperate to infiltrate your family set-up as soon as possible. Once inside, the Scorpio will instigate their own emotional hostile takeover, winning over key familial heads of state with their impeccable manners and rich back catalogue of anecdotes. While the Scorpio is always a hit with the parents, don't give up this family frontier easily: only show them yours if they show you theirs.

Best way to break up with a Scorpio: Tell them that you're polyamorous and want to share your love and body with the world. The Scorpio's highly jealous nature will render them paralysed by envy and suspicion, allowing you time to slip away. Delete their number and change your address.

(08:04): Fun night?

(10:44): Hey, there's no easy way to say this but I don't want to keep this from you any longer. I am polyamorous.

(10:46): WTF?

(10:47): Missed call
(10:48): Missed call
(10:51): Missed call

(10:52): WTF. Is this a joke? LOL. But seriously . . .

(10:57): Missed call

(12:14): It's not a joke. I want to share my love and body with the world, we are all deserving of everyone in this life.

(12:15): Missed call

(12:15): Seriously, WTF? How long has this been a thing? How many other people have there been?

(12:33): Missed call

(12:49): Missed call

(12:49): CALL ME BACK!

(13:19): HOW MANY OTHER PEOPLE!

(time delay)

(18:51): Sorry I freaked out just then. Just want to talk.

(19:22): Missed call

(19:27): Missed call

(19:31): I'M AT YOUR HOUSE. ANSWER THE DOOR.

(19:32): I've called the police. Please leave me alone.

'Number blocked'

A Scorpio's hall pass wish list

· · • ● • · ·

Dominic West

Miranda Priestly

Ryan Giggs

Ryan Giggs's brother's wife

Catherine the Great

SHAG/MARRY/AVOID

· · • ● • · ·

SHAG: *Cancer*

MARRY: *Capricorn*

AVOID: *Aquarius*

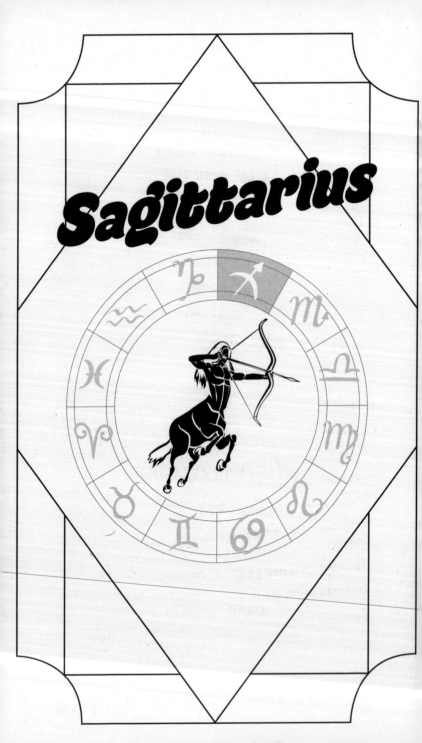

SAGITTARIUS

Sagittarius dates: 22 November – 21 December

Element: Fire

Ruling planet: Jupiter

Preferred pickup territory: Backpacker hostels

Attracted to: Four-day ayahuasca trips

One-night stand rating: 9/10

Favourite sex position: Side-saddle

Serial-killer vibes: 4/10

Introduces you to their parents: At the departure lounge

Potential ick-factor: 5/10

Preferred dating platform: Lonely Planet app

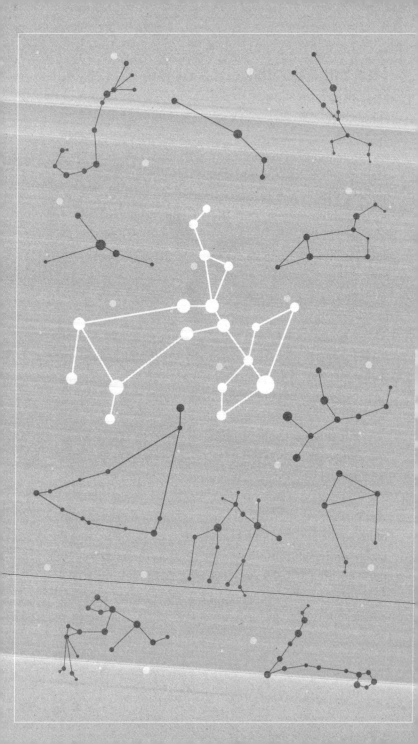

The Sagittarius:
Blessed by Jupiter and Mars, the Sagittarius is the most charmed house in all the zodiac. Positive and can-do, the Sagittarius is nothing but a ball of optimism and energy. This makes them company that everyone wants to keep. Smiley and silly, the Sagittarius is a fount of harmless fun and a harmless flirt as well. Their happy-go-lucky nature attracts many a suitor, though this is often unintentional. This results in many unsolicited advances but, true to their nature, few are turned away because life is there to be lived and Sagittarius is never one to turn down a new experience.

Depicted by the centaur, Saggis are the travellers of the zodiac, pilgrims on a quest to destination good-vibes. Armed with four legs and bow and arrow, like a trusty Land Rover they are prepared for any terrain. If you strike it up with a Sagittarius, be prepared to go off-piste, because their need to explore unfamiliar territory means that another adventure is only just around the corner.

While this is all undeniably thrilling, it does present some practical difficulties for prospective partners – largely because the Sagittarius refuses to sit still. Born with itchy feet and a pointy bottom, the Sagittarius has more vaccination passports than Chris Whitty and as many air miles as the entire population of Monaco. By definition, this makes dating a Sagittarius a fleeting affair. Fight this at your peril; become in any way clingy and demanding and the Sagittarius will ensure you never see them again. Step back and accept that some birds aren't meant to live in cages.

Shit where you eat? Why the hell not? After all, if you're cooped up with the same people day in day out in a nondescript office block, a cheeky bonk in the stationery cupboard is a sure-fire way to make the place more exciting. The Sagittarius has never been a stickler for the rules; in their eyes the red tape is there to be cut. You won't need to make the first move here – the Sagittarius will find you. This horny centaur will clip clop through the office in search of a sexual playmate. Once they've found you, set your Microsoft Teams status to 'busy' and let this wild horse drag you astray.

Typical profession: White-water rafting instructor.

The Sagittarius models themselves on: Bilbo Baggins or Dora the Explorer.

How to flirt with a Sagittarius: The Sagittarius needs to be kept on their toes. They want to be blindsided by spontaneous suggestions, challenges or left-field gossip. If you lead with 'How's work?' you could quickly find yourself having an early night, alone.

Preferred method of communication: Postcards, operating at a four-month delay.

The relationship history of a Sagittarius: Undefined. If you were a crime-scene investigator with a UV light, you'd be hard pushed to find a corner of the earth that

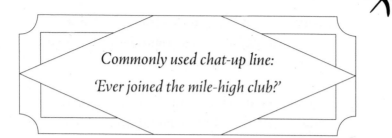

doesn't contain traces of their bodily fluids. They are international shaggers. Shaggitarius, if you will. From the Faroe Islands, to the streets of Bangcock (*sic*), the Sagittarius has spread their seed far and wide. They're the ones who get with the scuba-diving instructor, the hostel waiter and the customs inspector. They are by far the best to have around the table for a game of 'Never Have I Ever'. But while their sexual conquests are global in reach, few have ever materialized into anything substantial. This is exactly the way the Sagittarius wants it to be, and long may it continue.

Ideal first date with a Sagittarius: It's imperative that this takes place outdoors, for the Sagittarius comes alive in the presence of Mother Nature. A born wanderer, these stars were not built for four walls, so pack your compass, penknife, fanny pack and spork and be prepared to leave indoor plumbing behind. Suggest a day hiking out of town, go mudlarking along the river or walk the entirety of the M25 clockwise. The Sagittarius will be so thrilled to be out among the great outdoors, it will markedly improve the chances of them becoming enamoured with you.

For optimum results, begin dating a Sagittarius in May. The smells of spring – nettles, sap and petrichor – will whet their nasal passageways and have been known to prompt some serious al fresco activity.

N.B. If sexual acts in public areas aren't your thing, take the Sagittarius on a date to a climbing wall or a bouldering centre – these places were invented for them.

Split the bill? Nah, they will pick this up. The Sagittarius is a financial free spirit who lives in a mythical economic epoch of low regulation and 0 per cent interest rates. To their mind, it's always 2007 on Wall Street. Sit back and let the Sagittarius tap tap tap away.

How a Sagittarius will flirt with you: For the Sagittarius, flirting comes as easily as a fourteen-year-old watching OnlyFans. Their sunny disposition and infectious positivity is hard to resist and even harder not to interpret as something more than just matey. Matey is just how the Sagittarius gets their flirt on – expect plenty of joshing, pushing and tongue sticking outing. It's all a bit slapstick but in the best possible way. After all, who doesn't like a bit of pantomime?

Sexual appetite: Ravenous. Nowhere in life is the force of Jupiter more keenly felt by the Sagittarius than in the bedroom. Jupiter's exaggerated pull means that the Sagittarius is one of the most sexually orientated stars of the zodiac. Being the traveller of the galaxy, the Sagittarius loves exploring new frontiers and sees the body as a landscape waiting to be discovered. With a Sagittarius between your legs there is no map, no path, nor is there any return. Only possibilities await.

How to tell if a Sagittarius is into you: They put a finger up your bum.

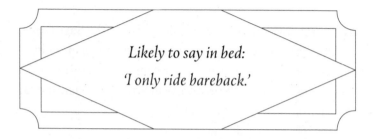

Likely to say in bed:
'I only ride bareback.'

Introduce to your parents: If you're tired of being called the square in the family.

Best way to break up with a Sagittarius: Get over-attached. Become a social limpet, an anxious barnacle, become cling film in human form. The Sagittarius will be so repulsed by this lack of independence that they will put you firmly in the bin.

(11:07): Hmmm what shall I have for my lunch?

(11:21): Quinoa or bulgur wheat? 🤔

(12:13): Hun?

(15:55): Have you seen it's raining?

(15:59): Shall I wear a jacket or just bring an umbrella? Also, what time are you gonna be done with work, as I might call ahead and book a table just in case. Do you think I should?

(18:02): I'm here early btw.

(18:26): I think your friend is here, too. Shall I go and say hi?

(18:30): I've warmed your seat for you! When are you getting here?

(18:31): I'm not.

Top 5 places to have sex with a Sagittarius

· · • ● • · ·

The Eden Project

During a long-haul flight

Halfway up a climbing wall

On camera

Anywhere in Yosemite

SHAG/MARRY/AVOID

· · • ● • · ·

SHAG: *Leo*

MARRY: *Aquarius*

AVOID: *Virgo*

CAPRICORN

η_o

Capricorn dates: 22 December – 19 January

Element: Earth

Ruling planet: Saturn

Preferred pickup territory: Conservative Party Conference

Attracted to: Durham University

One-night stand rating: 3/10

Favourite sex position: Missionary

Serial-killer vibes: 7/10

Introduces you to their parents after: Q2 of that financial year

Potential ick-factor: 5/10

Preferred dating platform: LinkedIn

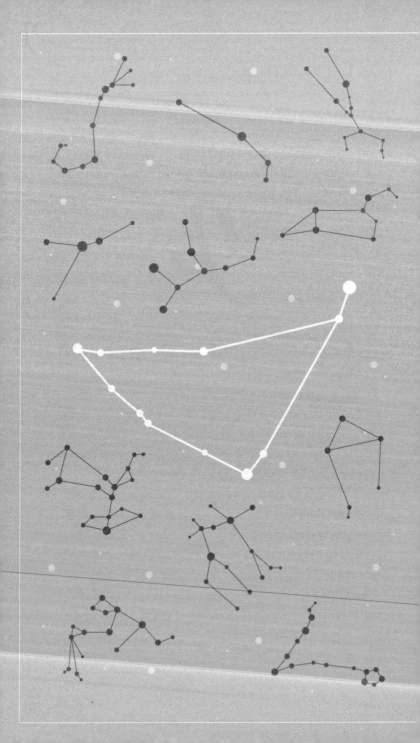

The Capricorn: Capricorns are ruled by the
stubborn spirit of the goat. But when it comes to dating, are
they really the GOAT?

Like Taurus and Virgo, Capricorns belong to the element
of earth. They are the green-and-yellow wire of the three-
point plug. And while being grounded is no bad thing,
the Capricorn's feet are rooted so firmly to the floor, it
makes levity nigh on impossible. This makes for a fun date!
Capricorns give off sensible eldest sibling vibes – they are
practical, serious, responsible – you get the picture. They're
a dry lunch, a German car, they leave helpful reviews on
Amazon, and if they could return to any point in history
they would probably elect to be a well-dressed civil servant
implementing George Osborne's austerity measures circa
2011. Ladies, please, form an orderly queue. And yes, you
guessed it, they love queueing.

Perhaps we're being unfair.

Ruled by Saturn, the Capricorn is a creature of order and
tradition. They're loyal and respectful and old-fashioned in
a cute(ish) kind of way. Think Mark Darcy meets Margaret
Thatcher. Capricorns can be cold and haven't always
been lucky in love. As a result, they have learned to love
themselves, perhaps a little too much. If you make it back
to a Capricorn's flat, check out the number of skincare
products in the bathroom and mirrors hanging on the walls.
There is a fine line between self-care and self-adoration.

Everything is very serious with Capricorns. If dating is
simply a recruitment session for sex, then a Capricorn's
interview process is no laughing matter and there are

multiple rounds. Don't be surprised if on a first date they ask you to describe a moment when you've had to overcome working with a difficult client and how you resolved the situation. This deadpan seriousness can be amusing, perhaps even ironic, and teasing them about this can be key to unlocking the Capricorn. But be warned: the joke only runs so deep. Dig a little deeper and you won't be surprised to find that most Capricorns are on the side of the boomers when it comes to the topics of today. Whatever you do, don't mention the war (on wokeism). With the pragmatic and sensible Capricorn, rarely are things given over to chance. A date with a Capricorn will be scheduled months in advance with clear start and finish times. If you think you might be out past ten p.m. on a school night, you can think again. Capricorns have their rules and they like sticking to them. While this can seem tedious and inflexible, Capricorns know what they want and what they stand for. If they choose to stand by you, they'll still be standing there until the end of your days.

Shit where you eat? Do you live to work or work to live? For the Capricorn, work equals life. Because at the end of the day we are not valued by our friends or family, but by the size of our bonus. Right? This is the gospel according to Capricorn.

Securing the attention of a Capricorn in the office is not an enviable task. While they may not be the sharpest tools in the shed, they are certainly one of the most industrious – a sturdy trowel, if you will. With their head-down, get-the-job-done approach, they can often be blind to the opportunities that lurk near by. Your only chance with a Capricorn is to learn to long it out, quite literally. These worker bees put in a shift like no other and are married to their desk eighteen hours a day. Your best bet for getting close to them is to learn to burn the midnight oil. Fire off some late-night Slack chat. Schedule some emails to send at 1:05 a.m. If you're not a night owl and would prefer to get a reasonable eight hours sleep, simply ask the office night porter to put in a good word for you.

P.S. The Capricorn may already be having an affair with the office night porter.

Typical profession: Partner at an accountancy firm or a senior traffic warden.

The Capricorn models themselves on: Anyone from HBO's *Industry*.

How to flirt with a Capricorn: The Capricorn will intend to make their status known to you from the very off. Their signature move, displaying their importance, authority and physical adherence to the work-life balance, is to place their *two* phones (one personal, one professional) on the table in front of you. They will extend you the courtesy of turning them face down and engage in some decidedly non-threatening eye contact while simultaneously perusing the wine list. This is now a status game. See them and raise them. Put down *three* phones. If you're feeling bold, throw in an iPad for good measure. The question 'Your place or mine?' will quickly follow.

Commonly used chat-up line:

'Paying 45 per cent tax is a real killer.'

Preferred method of communication: Microsoft Outlook.

The relationship history of a Capricorn: Extracting emotional information from a Capricorn can be like trying to speak to someone at Vodafone's customer services team. Capricorn's lack of availability comes from their ruling planet, Saturn. When the conversation of lovers past arises, Capricorns can quickly become cold and distant. Don't read into this too much. This speaks less to a gaping character flaw and more to the banal fact that typically Capricorns have very few previous lovers to talk about. Capricorns are solitary and responsible beings who don't give their heart away easily. If you find yourself on the receiving end of it, you might be the only one who ever does.

Ideal first date with a Capricorn: Nothing turns on a Capricorn more than status. Capitalism is their religion, and the Shard is their church. Suggest drinks on the thirty-second floor. The elevator trip alone will be their equivalent of a religious experience. By the fourth floor they will be

catching spirits and speaking in tongues. From here . . .
well, the rest is easy.

Split the bill? Capricorns like the finer things in life,
and they like letting you know that they can afford them.
They will take care of the bill but don't be surprised if they
make a meal out of doing so. Cue the flashing of multiple
American Express cards.

How a Capricorn will flirt with you: Capricorns
are notoriously stiff customers. Don't expect a volley of
friendly jibes, and whatever you do don't lead with any
gentle ribbing. Like an imported peach, the Capricorn's ego
bruises all too easily. But while Capricorns may be uptight,
they're not tight when it comes to their wallet and are
frequently spotted propping up the champagne and oyster
bar at Gatwick's South Terminal. If they start splashing the
cash, you'll know they deem you a worthy investment.

Sexual appetite: Tepid. Capricorn's pragmatic and
level-headed nature sadly travels into the bedroom. For

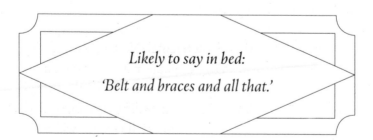

Likely to say in bed:
'Belt and braces and all that.'

the Capricorn, sex is like spontaneity or drinking on a Sunday – not something to be overindulged. Instead, it has a clearly defined purpose – to procreate and, on very special occasions, to relieve urges. Play up to the Capricorn's penchant for the material things in life, drop into conversation how much your designer underwear cost, and you'll find their urges might suddenly become all the more frequent.

How to tell if a Capricorn is into you: They invite you to their company away day.

Introduce to your parents: If you've got nothing better to do.

Best way to break up with a Capricorn: Tell them your ideal honeymoon would be spent protesting against economic inequality.

(09:41): Meeting booked with marriage registrar at 10 a.m. for Sunday. We can go to lunch with your rents after?

(09:56): Cool.

(09:56): I'll book somewhere.

(09:57): Also been thinking.

(10:00): 👀

(10:02): Maybe for our honeymoon we should camp out at an Occupy Wall St rally? There is one starting the day after the reception.

Notification (10:02):
'You have been removed from the group "Newlyweds"'

If dating is simply
a recruitment
session for sex,
then a Capricorn's
interview process is
no laughing matter

♑

A Capricorn's top 5 wedding venues

The Shard

Anywhere on Wall Street

The church where their father and their father's father and their father's father's father's father also got married

5 Hertford Street

The office

SHAG/MARRY/AVOID

SHAG: *Gemini*

MARRY: *Virgo*

AVOID: *Aquarius*

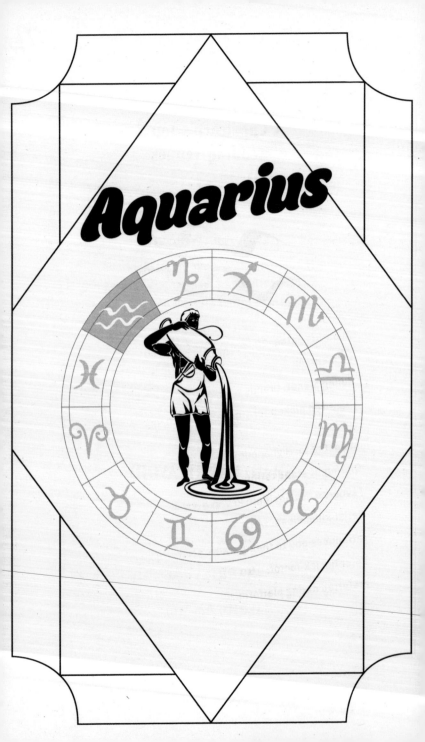

AQUARIUS

Aquarius dates: 20 January – 18 February

Element: Air

Ruling planet: Uranus

Preferred pickup territory: Climate change conference

Attracted to: Higher purposes

One-night stand rating: 7/10

Favourite sex position: Reverse cowgirl

Serial-killer vibes: 1/10

Introduces you to their parents after: 2 years

Potential ick-factor: 3/10

Preferred dating platform: IRL

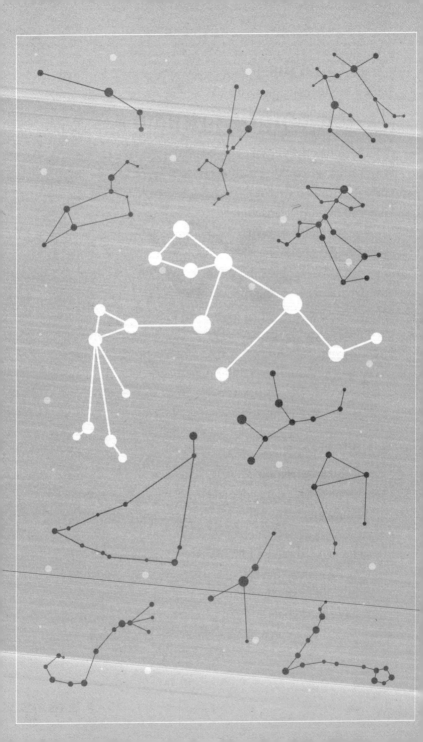

The Aquarius: Immortalized by the giddy harmonies of The 5th Dimension's 1969 smash hit, 'Aquarius', the age of Aquarius promises an era of harmony, prosperity and peace. And while we technically should have entered this period at the vernal equinox in March 2021, it's fair to say that we couldn't be further away from that spiritual promised land if we tried. Which begs the question: where have all the Aquarians gone?

Don't bother furiously swiping through the apps, you won't find them on there. No, the Aquarius would never flock to those soulless digital cattle markets to find love – they're too busy saving the world, and maybe finding a bae along the way.

The Aquarius is the individual of the zodiac: they're the middle child, the family vegan, the village horse whisperer. In short, the Aquarius is different. Governed by the element of air, they are free spirits, floating through the galaxy on a mission known only to them. But make no mistake, the Aquarius is no airhead. Blessed with fierce intelligence and insight, the Aquarius is awake to all the problems of the world and is determined to solve them by any means they can. If you're on a date with an Aquarius, you'd better be up for joining their cause. If you're not, you will be by the end of it. There is a reason so many notable leaders belong to this star sign: Abraham Lincoln, President Zelensky, Kim Jong-il. Read into that last one what you will.

This is not to say that all Aquarians are dictators, but they have fixed goals and see the beaten track as the path of the coward. This can make dating an Aquarius a tricky task

– trying to pin them down can be akin to placing a tracking device a white rhino. But if you do manage to land your dart in their heart then you've struck gold, for the Aquarius is like no other. Their ruling planet of Uranus (come on, you're better than that) means there is never a dull moment, particularly in bed. If you're prepared to open your eyes, as well as your heart, then the Aquarius will show you the dawn of the new age.

Shit where you eat? The factory settings for an Aquarius are always to see the bigger picture. To them, a job without purpose is not a job worth doing. Naturally, this rules out vast swathes of potential employment opportunities and is the reason why most Aquarians end up working for an NGO. While their profession is entwined with their moral social conscience, this doesn't rule out their sexual consciousness. Just don't be surprised if they bring their white helmet to bed with you, for in the bedroom the Aquarius is *sans frontières*.

Typical profession: Tattoo artist or field agent for Amnesty International.

The Aquarius models themselves on: Any protagonist from any Sally Rooney novel.

How to flirt with an Aquarius: Nothing turns on an Aquarius more than intellectual stimulation. Exploit this to your advantage. As you arrive on your date, make sure your copy of Susan Sontag is visibly well thumbed and on display. Remove your headphones but ensure the volume is high enough so they can just catch the middle eight of Nick Cave's latest track before politely stowing them away. Apologize for being late. The queer performance poetry recital you just attended slightly overran. They will forgive you instantly. Remember, the Aquarius is looking for their intellectual equal first and a one-night stand second. As the conversation moves on, feel free to drop in some bigger hitters: tell them about the time you interned at a podcast production company in the Gaza Strip or suggest going to that twenty-four-hour installation at the Barbican that no one else wants to go to. Show them how many thumbs-ups your review of Pedro Almodóvar's latest film received on Rotten Tomatoes. All of this will be catnip to the Aquarius. Deploy the correct pronunciation of Proust and they'll pounce on you there and then.

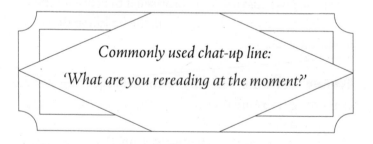

Commonly used chat-up line:
'What are you rereading at the moment?'

Preferred method of communication: Verbal. And loquacious.

The relationship history of an Aquarius: There is no easy answer to this question and you should never expect anything so crude as a body count. The Aquarius's ruling element of the air means that people come and go in their life just as a leaf gets carried on the breeze. This isn't to say that these connections aren't meaningful, but rather they are numerous and fleeting – as they have to be – while the Aquarius marches on to the beat of their purposeful drum.

Ideal first date with an Aquarius: Anything in Margate. The Aquarius will feel the spiritual pull of Tracey Emin's home town and will immediately feel at one here. No one will blink at their fashion choices, and the stark disparities in the socio-economic fortunes of the local community, caused by the tightening grip of gentrification, will provide a suitably profound and concerning backdrop against which to enjoy your fish and chips.

Split the bill? To the Aquarius, a bill is just a number and they firmly believe that what goes around comes around. You might find yourself on the sharp end of this philosophy. Book in a second date to test if their theory holds water.

How an Aquarius will flirt with you: They'll invite you to a protest. Here are the top five sexy causes the Aquarius likes to march to:

- 'Free the nipple!'
- 'Defrost Walt Disney!'
- 'Gingers have souls!'
- 'Release more serotonin!'

•• 'Bring back the bush!'

Sexual appetite: Medium. It's not that the Aquarius doesn't like sex, or that they aren't any good at it (they're better than most), but rather their head is elsewhere. For the Aquarius, there are more important current events than what's going on down there.

Likely to say in bed: 'Did you know that globally one in three people don't have access to safe drinking water?'

How to tell if an Aquarius is into you: As a free spirit, the Aquarius is allergic to labels. It's not uncommon for an Aquarius to say after two years of a relationship that they are still just 'seeing' you. If they ever DTR and introduce you as their partner, you'll know you have them hooked.

Introduce to your parents: By way of a publicly backed petition north of a thousand signatures.

Best way to break up with an Aquarius: Tell them you think climate change is a myth. They will cancel you then and there. You will never hear from them again.

(22:36): DW, back home. Wanna do something later this week?

(13:49): Hello?

(14:29): Hey sorry for the slow reply. Been thinking a lot about the Al Gore link you sent. I'm not sure I buy it. If you look at the carbon cycles over millennia, this is totally normal. I seriously think everyone needs to just chill out, no?

Notification (14:30): 'Your number has been blocked.'

5 ways to propose to an Aquarius

• • ● • •

While clearing mines in post-war Kosovo

With a compostable ring, whittled out of wild horsehair

Halfway through a three-day transcendental meditation session

By hiding a ring in the pages of a second-hand Simone de Beauvoir novel

Anywhere in Margate

SHAG/MARRY/AVOID

• • ● • •

SHAG: *Sagittarius*

MARRY: *Libra*

AVOID: *Leo*

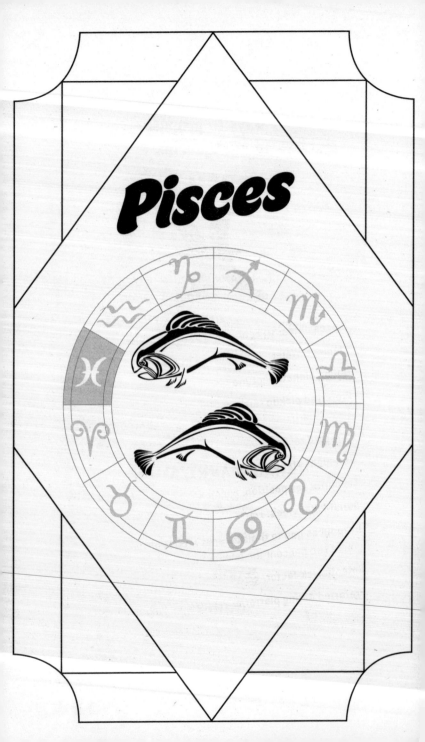

PISCES

Pisces dates: 19 February – 20 March

Element: Water

Ruling planet: Neptune

Preferred pickup territory: The Healing Field, Glastonbury

Attracted to: Goop

One-night stand rating: 5/10

Favourite sex position: Flying fish

Serial-killer vibes: 1/10

Introduces you to their parents after: Deciding you're 100 per cent the one for them

Potential ick-factor: 3/10

Preferred dating platform: Plenty More Fish

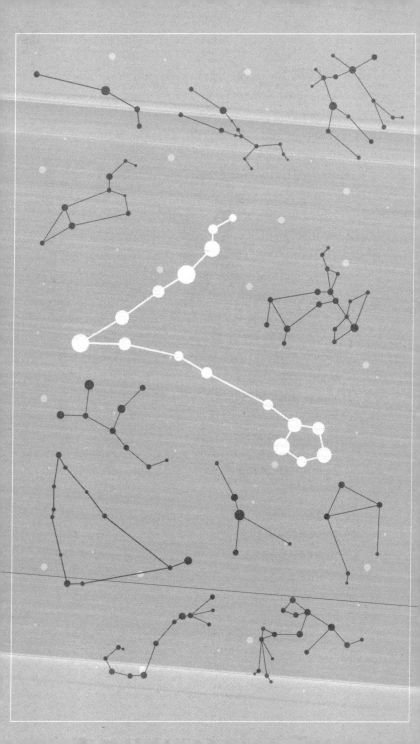

The Pisces: The twelfth sign of the zodiac, the Pisces is perhaps the most perceptive and intuitive of all the stars. With its ruling planets of Jupiter and Neptune, the Pisces is generous and sensitive; the shoulder we turn to cry on when our stars just don't seem to align.

Characterized by two fish swimming in different directions, their totem symbolizes the eternal conflict of their character – the battle between their head and their heart. This can make the Pisces a rather slippery fish when it comes to the world of dating. The conflicting elements of air and water mean that the Pisces mind is a SodaStream of frothy indecision, constantly trying to figure out whether to stick or twist, leave or remain. One minute they are planning to move in with you, the next wanting to be a single Pringle playing the field. Going out with a Pisces can be a wild ride and not the most settling of experiences. Their idealistic nature means they always believe the water is warmer elsewhere. It's your job to remind them that while this might be the case, the Great Barrier Reef is now a bleached wasteland of nothingness and despair and they're far better off staying here with you.

But for all their inner umming and erring, in the end the Pisces always follows their gut. If you want the Pisces to follow you, make sure you've got some kimchi and Yakult to hand. Without doubt, Pisces are special creatures – they are the dreamers and the visionaries whose world view and understanding is second to none. In short, they are a catch. If you find one slipping through the net, think twice about letting it go. There might be plenty more fish in the sea, but there aren't many like the Pisces.

Shit where you eat? When it comes to the career of a Pisces, they know that their time on this planet is not meant to be spent in the pursuit of profit. It's about connecting with people and making a meaningful difference. They don't care about the bottom line of a balance sheet; they care about what goes on between the bed sheets. You have nothing to lose, so ask.

Typical profession: Art therapist or founder of a sustainable microbrewery selling kelp-infused kombucha drinks.

The Pisces models themselves on: Philippa Perry.

How to flirt with a Pisces: The Pisces' inherently conflicted nature means they're often guilty of giving off mixed signals. One minute they're hot, the next, oh so cold. They can go from stroking your leg beneath exposed-bulb lighting to giving you the cold shoulder on a dark street corner. Your job is to try to master their conflicting forces, leaving no room for doubt in their mind. Play up to their planetary prejudices towards vulnerability and compassion:

- Show them the in-app trophies you've accumulated on Headspace
- Talk about the ex you've yet to get over and perhaps never will

- Show them the results of your Tuesday-night pottery classes

- Start crying. Nothing turns on a Pisces more than those salty, salty tears

Commonly used chat-up line:

My mind is telling me NOOO, but my body is telling me YAAAS!

Preferred method of communication: Telepathy.

The relationship history of a Pisces: The Pisces are lovers of love. Their open heart and empathetic nature means they are no strangers to being in love, although not always with the star pupils. Their patience, compassion and curiosity for connection has often led them to people whom others would run a mile from. There is a reason why there are lots of Pisces' exes in prison. And while the state may have found them guilty, in the eyes of the Pisces they will always be innocent. Don't be surprised if you find yourself accompanying a Pisces to HMP Pentonville to check in on an old friend. You've nothing to fear – they are not getting out any time soon.

Ideal first date with a Pisces: The Pisces' creative and imaginative nature means they won't be impressed if you play this one straight. A simple trip to the pub and three pints isn't going to cut the mustard. You need to think outside the box – take them life drawing, try your hand at falconry, go and visit their ancestor's grave. Failing that, invite them lucid dreaming – a trip into your subconscious will get them chomping at the bit. Just make sure you've cleared up your Oedipus complex before you take them there.

Split the bill? Financial flexing isn't going to score you any points, so stop your insisting and just split it fifty-fifty.

How a Pisces will flirt with you: Flirting is not something that comes naturally to a Pisces. Cheeky winks and cocked eyebrows are alien expressions to their facial muscles. Instead, the Pisces wants to connect on a deeper level; they want to make sure that if they're taking you home, they're taking home the *real* you. Keep an eye out for penetrating questions about your past, your fears, your sexual inadequacies. While this may feel like being emotionally waterboarded, it's much more altruistic. This is the Pisces way of forming a connection with you. If you're open to their line of questioning, they'll quickly open right up for you.

Sexual appetite: Expansive. Ruled by Neptune, the celestial orb of dreams and imaginings, the Pisces has always had question marks over the rules and boundaries we set for ourselves. This is not to say they're the chaos maker or the *enfant terrible* of the zodiac; rather, their accumulated wisdom has led them to thoughtfully challenge all that we know. This feeds into the bedroom. The word 'taboo' does not feature in the Pisces dictionary. Our bodies are there to be explored and no one, no thing and nowhere is off limits. So be prepared: if you aren't open to exploring uncharted waters, you may quickly find this fish going cold on you.

Likely to say in bed: 'Yes! Right there! That's my soul!'

How to tell if a Pisces is into you: They will engage you in intense bouts of PDA, aggressively leaning into the P aspect of this acronym.

Introduce to your parents: Only if you're sure. The Pisces will see this as a huge moment in your relationship. For them, this is their Big Bang. No pressure.

Best way to break up with a Pisces: You won't need to. They will already know the way your heart is headed.

(14:19): Hey, I think we need to talk.

(14:19): Hey, I think we need to talk.

(14:20): Jinx!

(14: 20): Gah!

(14:21): I get it, don't sweat it. Take care x

5 questions a Pisces will ask you on a first date

•••●••

So how's your relationship with your father?

Do you ever think that monogamy is just a vice constructed by society to tighten its grip on our capitalist psyche?

A pint is quite a lot of liquid, isn't it?

I wonder if people ever do truly know me, you know?

Wait, did you wash your hands?

SHAG/MARRY/AVOID

••●●••

SHAG: *Capricorn*

MARRY: *Cancer*

AVOID: *Gemini*

Acknowledgements

My never-ending thanks to Sharika Teelwah, Laura Williams, Marianne Issa El-Khoury, Col, Sophie McVeigh, Phil Lord, Phil Evans, Barbara Thompson and Lily Pickard, who made this happen and together make up the finest constellation in the publishing galaxy.

I would like to thank the night porters at the Royal Observatory, Greenwich for allowing me to use their telescopes after hours, without which my understanding of the night sky would remain murky at best.

I'm deeply indebted to the following establishments, which have been home to too many first dates and where the key research for this book was undertaken: the John Snow, Soho; Skeeter's Axe Throwing in Hackney Wick; Zoom; Gordon's Wine Bar, Embankment; Santander Cycles; Radisson Blu (multiple locations).

Lastly, I'm forever grateful to all those who accompanied me there. I hope these pages provide something of an explanation. This book is for you.

About the Author

B. J. Lovegood is an amateur astrologer, accountant and speed-dating enthusiast. Their writing has been cited in multiple Reddit threads and they are an unofficial patron of the nudist-stargazing society. They live off-grid.